Home Maths Ages 10–11

Anita Straker

CAMBRIDGE
UNIVERSITY PRESS

Ask an adult to time you.

You need pencil and paper. Write only the answers.

1 $56 \div 8$.

2 $67 + 84$.

3 $6006 - 4987$.

4 80×30.

5 5^2.

6 Write **20 007** in words.

7 Write all the factors of 12.

8 10% of 30.

9 Take 100m from 5km.

10 $85 + \square = 143$.

11 Approximately, what is 78×38?

12 $\frac{9}{10}$ of £20.

13 Find the average of 36 and 94.

14 $80 \times 52 = 4160$. What is 80×26?

2

Prime down

Two, three or four people can play.

You need some beans.

The first player chooses a starting number between 50 and 500.

Take turns.

You can **either** double the number **or** subtract a prime number.

The first player to reach zero exactly wins a bean.

> **2, 3, 5, 7, 11, 13 … and so on are prime numbers.**
>
> **A prime number has exactly two factors: itself and 1.**

Play lots of times. Take turns to go first.

The winner is the player who gets the most beans.

Recognise prime numbers
Double and subtract two- or three-digit numbers

Holidays

Ask all your family to join in.

You may need a calculator.

$$\text{H} \quad \text{O} \quad \text{L} \quad \text{I} \quad \text{D} \quad \text{A} \quad \text{Y} \quad \text{S}$$
$$\textbf{2} \quad \textbf{3} \quad \textbf{4} \quad \textbf{5} \quad \textbf{6} \quad \textbf{7} \quad \textbf{8} \quad \textbf{9}$$

Multiply the numbers standing for the letters.

Find two-letter words or three-letter words that are worth these.

1	18	**5**	80	**9**	180
2	63	**6**	120	**10**	168
3	45	**7**	60	**11**	126
4	27	**8**	90	**12**	112

Secretly make another word using the letters of HOLIDAYS.

Work out what it is worth and tell everyone.

Can they guess what your word is?

Multiply two or three numbers up to 9
Use times tables and short multiplication

Number race

Play with a partner.

You need to see a clock or watch with a second hand.

You need some beans and a pack of playing cards.

Use the ace to 10 of each suit.

Take turns to go first.

Shuffle the cards and put the pack face down.

The first player chooses a target number and says 'Go'.

The target must be between 20 and 60.

The second player takes five cards from the pack.

Use the five cards to make the target number.

Use each number once and only once and any operation (+, −, × or ÷).

If the target is, say, 32 and you have 2, 3, 4, 5 and 7, you could do

$$(7 \times 3) + 5 + 4 + 2 \quad \text{or} \quad (35 - 27) \times 4$$

If the target is made in under 2 minutes the second player wins a bean.

Otherwise the first player wins a bean.

Have five turns each.

The winner of the game is the player with most beans.

Use knowledge of number facts and times-tables
Think flexibly and eliminate what won't work

Ask an adult to read you these.

You need pencil and paper. Write only the answers.

1 Take 14 from 9 plus 7.

2 Eleven fives.

3 700 times 40.

4 One tenth of 1 kilogram.

5 What fraction of £5 is 50p?

6 63 divided by 7.

7 Three tenths of 80.

8 Write 0.5 litres in millilitres.

9 How many hours in 3 days?

10 Take two thirds from 2.

11 75 per cent of 20.

12 Take £12.81 from £20.

13 Divide 97 by 10.

14 Write 33⅓ per cent as a fraction.

You need pencil and paper. Write only the answers.

1 86 taken from a number leaves 47. What is the number?

2 Andover to London is 78 miles. How far is it there and back?

3 How long is it from 7:37 a.m. to 8:20 a.m?

4 Approximately, what is 72 x 68?

5 Dad is 35 cm short of 2 metres. How tall is he?

6 Add 500 ml to three-quarters of 1 litre.

7 A number divided by 7 gives 36. What is the number?

8 What is the area of a 14 cm by 20 cm rectangle?

9 Write **three hundredths** as a decimal.

10 How many 250 g pots of jam can be filled from a 5 kg container?

Addition puzzle

Do this by yourself.

You need pencil and paper.

Copy and complete this addition table.

+	34		25		16
19	53				
		66		86	
	87	71			
					53
				64	

Add or subtract pairs of two-digit numbers
Work out a strategy

Ask an adult to time you.

You need pencil and paper. Write only the answers.

1   500 times 50.

2   157 – 82.

3   10% of 1 kilometre.

4   Write **40 600** in words.

5   Share 42 equally among 6.

6   Find the average of 13, 17 and 27.

7   25% of £80.

8   Take 17.28 metres from 20 metres.

9 $15 \times 16 = 240$. What is 15×17?

10   Take 10 grams from 1 kilogram.

11   Write all the factors of 42.

12 $122 - \square = 53$.

13   ¾ of 28.

14   Divide 23 by 100.

Where does it go?

Do this by yourself.

You need pencil and paper.

Draw this grid.

	even	divisible by 3	divisible by 5	prime
odd				
less than 15				
square				
divisible by 6				
divisible by 4				

Make a list of the numbers 2 to 30.

Write each of the numbers 2 to 30 in a suitable box on the grid.

You can write some numbers in more than one box.

Cross the number off your list when you have written it on the grid.

Two of the numbers will not fit in a box. Which are they?

Some boxes will stay empty. Discuss with your family why this is.

Recognise properties of numbers 1 to 30
Work systematically

Letter lines

Start this on your own.

You need paper, a pencil and some scissors.

Make 9 number cards.

Arrange your cards in the shapes of the letters.

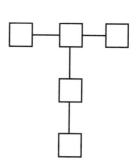

a.   Use the cards 1 to 5.

Make each line add up to 8.

Make each line add up to 9.

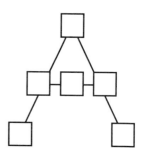

b.   Use the cards 1 to 6.

Make each line of A add to 9.

Make each line add up to 10.

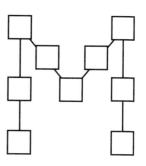

c.   Use the cards 1 to 9.

Make each line of M add to 14.

Make each line add up to 16.

Record each solution but keep it secret.

Now ask your family to try.

Add several small numbers
Think logically to eliminate what won't work

You need pencil and paper. Write only the answers.

1   What must you divide 400 by to get 16?

2   Twice a number is 16 less than 40. What is the number?

3   Bananas cost 55p for 8. How much do 40 bananas cost?

4   What is the volume of a 5 cm by 6 cm by 7 cm cuboid?

5   1 kg of tea costs £2.40. What is the cost of a 250 g packet ?

6   The perimeter of a square is 12 metres. What is its area?

7   How many 19p notebooks can you buy for £5?

8   What number taken from 64 leaves 27?

9   Approximately, what is 282 ÷ 41?

10 How many bags of 25 daffodil bulbs
        can be filled from a sack of 1003?

Ask an adult to read you these.
You need pencil and paper. Write only the answers.

1   Take seven tenths from 2.

2   Divide 3 by 10.

3   59 plus 97.

4   Double 275.

5   900 times 70.

6   Three quarters of 1000.

7   683 take away 15.

8   Find the product of 6, 7 and 20.

9   Take 50 millilitres from 1 litre.

10 Add two fifths to four fifths.

11 Write 75 per cent as a decimal.

12 8 pens at 59p each cost … ?

13 How many minutes in 7 hours?

14 How many vertices has a cube?

Ask an adult to time you.

You need pencil and paper. Write only the answers.

1 $85 \div 5$.

2 $\square \times 7 = 357$.

3   Write **10 010** in words.

4   Write all the factors of 16.

5 $^4\!/_5$ of 30.

6   Take 9 mm from 5 cm.

7   Round 6092 to the nearest 100.

8   75% of £120.

9 $49 \div 21$.

10 $\frac{1}{2} \times \frac{1}{2}$.

11   £39.17 − £17.25.

12   Double 385.

13   Divide 7 by 100.

14 $64 \times 8 = 512$. What is 64×16?

14

Kite puzzle

This kite is made up of lots of triangles.

Some of them are inside others.

How many of them can you count?

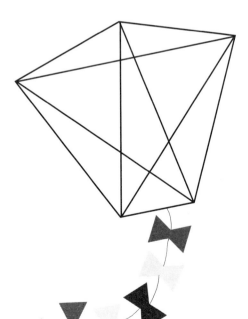

Ask your family and friends to try.

Can they find as many triangles as you can?

Recognise triangles
Work out a strategy

Know when to stop

Two, three or four people can play.

You need two dice.

Each player needs pencil and paper.

Each player starts with a score of zero.

Take turns to roll the two dice as many times as you like.

Each time multiply the two numbers you roll.

Add the product to your previous total and write it on your paper.

Choose when to end your turn.

Beware – if you roll a 6 your score on that turn is wiped out!

If you roll double 6 your total score from all turns is wiped out!

The first to get to 250 wins.

Change the rules

a.   Subtract your scores from 500.

b.   Roll 3 dice and aim to reach 1000.

Practise times-tables up to 6 × 6
Keep a running total of one- or two-digit numbers

Summit talk

Two, three or four people can play.

You need a pack of playing cards.

Use the ace to 9 of each suit.

Each player needs pencil and paper.

Shuffle the cards.

Deal 6 cards to each player.

Use the cards to make two products.

Work out your two products. Add them together.

The player with the largest total scores a point.

Return the cards to the pack, shuffle them and deal again.

The winner is the first player to get 10 points.

Change the rules

a.   The player with the smallest sum scores a point.

b.   Make the two products

☐☐ × ☐☐ and ☐ × ☐.

Practise short multiplication; add two- or three digit numbers
Understand place value and work out a strategy

Ask an adult to read you these.
You need pencil and paper. Write only the answers.

1 66 minus 8.

2 Halve 312.

3 Add 68 to 88.

4 25 less than 79.

5 Write 25 per cent as a decimal.

6 Two fifths of 60.

7 Subtract 45 from 195.

8 Find the total of 8, 3, 7 and 2.

9 Share 92 equally among 4.

10 What is the square root of 36?

11 Take 40 metres from 2 kilometres.

12 What number added to 55 gives 82?

13 Multiply 48 by 3.

14 6000 divided by 100.

You need pencil and paper. Write only the answers.

1 It is 4:48 p.m. What time will it be half an hour from now?

2 8 kilometres is about 5 miles. About how many miles is 48 km?

3 How many ½ litre jugs does it take to fill a 10 litre bucket?

4 A plane flies 1200 miles in 3 hours. What is its average speed?

5 A ride at the fair costs £1.85. How much is it for 3 rides?

6 Write in order, smallest first: 1.5, 2.1, 0.9, 1.7.

7 How many quarters in 12½?

8 How many edges has a cube?

9 Divide 60 into 3000.

10 How much does the flour weigh?

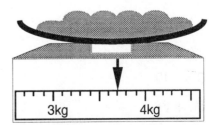

19

Try these by yourself.

You need pencil and paper.

Winston's homework has got splashed.

Each ❄ is where the water went on a digit.

Help him by copying and completing these.

a. $4❄ + ❄8 = ❄44$

b. $7❄ - ❄9 = 24$

c. $❄2❄ \times 7 = 1❄7❄$

d. $❄9❄ \div 6 = ❄4❄$

Use knowledge of number facts and times-tables
Think logically and eliminate what won't work

20

Ask an adult to time you.

You need pencil and paper. Write only the answers.

1 $\square \div 8 = 52$.

2 $154 - 86$.

3   Subtract 36 cm from 2 m.

4   5% of 200.

5 $2\frac{1}{4} - 1\frac{3}{4}$.

6 0.5×10.

7 $1\frac{2}{3} + 1\frac{2}{3}$.

8   How many days in 2 years?

9   Round 9957 to the nearest 100.

10   Write all the factors of 30.

11   Approximately, what is $299 \div 11$?

12   One tenth of £7.50.

13   What is the square root of 81?

14 $5 \times 47 = 235$. What is 5×48?

Three card tricks

Three or four people can play.

Each player needs pencil and paper.

You need a pack of playing cards.

Use cards 2 to 10 of each suit.

Shuffle the cards and place the pack face down.

Take turns to take three cards.

Use your three numbers in any combination to get your score.

You must only use addition or multiplication.

With, say, 7, 3 and 8, you could make any of these.

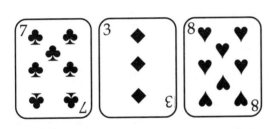

$$7 + 3 + 8 = 18$$
$$7 \times 3 + 8 = 29$$
$$7 \times 8 + 3 = 59$$
$$8 \times 3 + 7 = 31$$
$$7 \times 3 \times 8 = 168$$

Write your score from that turn on your paper.

Have five turns each.

The winner is the player whose total score is nearest to 300.

Change the rules

a.   Use any of the four rules (+, −, × or ÷).

b.   Choose a different total score to aim for.

Use knowledge of number facts and times-tables
Think flexibly and eliminate what won't work

Rounding

Play with a partner.

You need pencil and paper between you.

Draw this grid.

20	140	40	110	60
200	340	290	410	630
880	560	90	440	800
250	430	320	370	210
70	160	50	130	30

Take turns to choose two of these numbers and multiply them.

Round the product to the nearest 10.

If it is on the grid, mark it with your initial.

Each number on the grid can be marked only once.

If there is no new number to mark, wait for your next turn.

The winner is the first to get four of their initials in a straight line.

The line can be horizontal, vertical or diagonal.

Play several times.

Practise long or short multiplication
Round to the nearest 10 and work out a strategy

You need pencil and paper. Write only the answers.

1 Half a number is 18 more than 25. What is the number?

2 Apples cost 48p for 6. How much do 5 apples cost?

3 It is 11:18 p.m. What time was it 45 minutes ago?

4 42% of a pattern is red. What percentage is not red?

5 What is the remainder when 500 is dived by 70?

6 1 litre is about 1¾ pints. About how many pints is 3 litres?

7 How many faces has a square-based pyramid?

8 Write **one million and eighty** in figures.

9 Approximately, what is 2990 ÷ 59?

10 A car's average speed is 50 m.p.h. How far does it go in 2½ hours?

Ask an adult to read you these.
You need pencil and paper. Write only the answers.

1 Two cubed.

2 Divide 7 by 100.

3 Eleven squared.

4 5 per cent of 60.

5 600 times 800.

6 Divide 2.8 by 7.

7 Add 37p to £1.90.

8 Find the difference between 7.2 and 4.7.

9 Write 473 centimetres in metres.

10 Find the average of 19 and 26.

11 Write 30 per cent as a fraction.

12 One eighth of 1000.

13 What is the square root of 144?

14 What number taken from 2 leaves 0.3?

Ask an adult to time you.

You need pencil and paper. Write only the answers.

1 0.5×10.

2   Double 195.

3   Decrease 81 by 38.

4 $4 + \square + 15 = 26$.

5   Roughly, what is $698 \div 7$?

6 12^2.

7   Add 10 to –4.

8   Subtract ⅓ from 3.

9 $5.6 + 6.5$.

10   Write 0.8 as a fraction.

11   One fifth of 90.

12 $6 + 8 + 9 + 5$.

13 $600 \div 4$.

14   Write the product of 6, 7 and 20.

26

Sort them out

Do this by yourself.

You need pencil and paper.

Copy and complete this diagram.

Numbers from 100 to 150

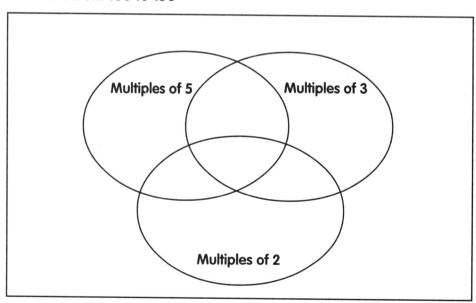

Snakes

Play this with a partner who has a calculator.

You may need pencil and paper.

S N A K E   P I T

2   3   4   5   6   7   8   9

Each letter has a value.

Multiply the numbers in the words below. Try to do this in your head.

Your partner should check and say if you are right.

1	P E N	**5**	A S K	**9**	E A T	**13**	P E T
2	S E A	**6**	S E T	**10**	T I N	**14**	T A P
3	N E T	**7**	I N K	**11**	P E A	**15**	P I N
4	I N N	**8**	P A N	**12**	K I T	**16**	T I P

Think of more words using the letters of SNAKE PIT.

Ask your partner to work out what they are worth.

You must say if your partner is right.

Find the products of two or more numbers
Use times-tables facts

Make one

Ask all your family to join in.

Each person needs pencil and paper.

17 can become 1 using only the digit 3 and any operation ($+$, $-$, $\times$ or $\div$).

Each of these examples takes 5 steps.

17	$\times$ 3	=	51
	$-$ 33	=	18
	$\div$ 3	=	6
	$-$ 3	=	3
	$\div$ 3	=	1

17	$-$ 3	=	14
	$\times$ 3	=	42
	$-$ 33	=	9
	$\div$ 3	=	3
	$\div$ 3	=	1

Change 17 to 1 using only the digit 4 and any operation.

Who can do it first?

Who takes fewest steps?

Now change 17 to 1 using only the digit 5 and any operation.

What about using only the digit 6?

Or the digit 2?

Change the rules

a. Change 19 to 1 using only the digit 2, or 3, or 4, or 5, or 6 …

b. Choose some other numbers and try to change them to 1.

Use knowledge of number facts and times-tables
Think flexibly and eliminate what won't work

Ask an adult to read you these.
You need pencil and paper. Write only the answers.

1   Three cubed.

2   67 minus 48, plus 6.

3   Divide 126 by 21.

4   50% of 90 millilitres.

5   Take 88 from 105.

6   Twice 57.

7   Is 368 a multiple of 4?

8   What is the square root of 121?

9   Double the sum of 17 and 18.

10   Increase £100 by 10 per cent.

11   Write 0.6 as a fraction.

12   Subtract 4.9 from 8.1.

13   What fraction of £10 is £2?

14   How many 20p coins make £60?

You need pencil and paper. Write only the answers.

1   What is the difference between 73 and 200?

2   Write in order, smallest first: $\frac{3}{5}$, $\frac{1}{2}$, $\frac{3}{4}$, $\frac{1}{5}$.

3   60% of a class of 30 are girls. How many boys are there in the class?

4   How much change from £5 for 6 ices at 75p each?

5   What must be added to –15 to make 30?

6   If 37 nines are 333, what are 38 nines?

7   How many faces has a cuboid?

8   How many hours in 5 days?

9   How many tenths in 4½?

10   Take 10% off £80.

In the cave

Try this by yourself.

You may need pencil and paper.

Some beetles and tarantulas live in a cave.

There are 100 of them altogether.

Together they have 650 legs.

How many beetles are there? How many tarantulas?

Make up another puzzle like this. Can someone in your family do it?

Recognise then add multiples of 6 and 8
Work out a strategy

32

Ask an adult to time you.

You need pencil and paper. Write only the answers.

1 Half of three-quarters.	**8** $4 \times \square \times 5 = 60$.
2 0.09 x 10.	**9** Roughly, what is $597 \div 4$?
3 Add 130 to 421.	**10** Write 0.4 as a percentage.
4 1000 – 976.	**11** Find the average of 8, 7 and 6.
5 $\frac{1}{20}$ of 60.	**12** What fraction of 24 is 9?
6 $587 + \square = 606$.	**13** 52 times 8.
7 One tenth of £8.50.	**14** What fraction of 20 kg is 4 kg?

Tiggy in the middle

Two, three or four people can play.

You need a pack of playing cards.

Use the ace to 10 of each suit.

Shuffle the cards.

Turn the top card face up and put it in the middle of the table.

Deal everyone four cards.

Use your four cards to make the number in the middle.

You can use some or all of your cards and any operation (+, −, × or ÷).

The first to make the middle number calls out 'Tiggy' and collects that card.

Return all the other cards to the pack, shuffle and deal again.

The winner is the first to collect 10 cards.

Change the rules

a. Turn over two cards and make a two-digit number for the middle.

b. Deal everyone five cards.

Use knowledge of number facts and times-tables
Think flexibly and eliminate what won't work

At the zoo

Do this by yourself.

You need pencil and paper.

The names of 8 animals are hidden in this puzzle.

To find them, follow a continuous track once through every square.

You can move up, down or sideways but not diagonally.

C	F	W	N	P	A
A	L	O	O	E	L
M	E	L	I	L	A
X	O	F	E	M	E
B	E	A	R	U	S

Each letter has a value. A is 1, B is 2, C is 3, and so on.

You will need to work out the rest.

Add up the numbers in the animals' names.

Which animals have these totals?

a. 22   c. 34   e. 39   g. 45

b. 26   d. 37   f. 56   h. 50

Add several one- and two-digit numbers

Home Maths Ages 10–11 Answers

1
1. 7
2. 151
3. 1019
4. 2400
5. 25
6. twenty thousand and seven
7. 1, 12   2, 6   3, 4
8. 3
9. 4.9 kilometres (4.9km), or 4900 metres (4900m)
10. 58
11. 3200
12. £18
13. 65
14. 2080

3
1. 18   DO
2. 63   AS
3. 45   IS
4. 27   SO
5. 80   ILL
6. 120 LID
7. 60   OIL, HID
8. 90   HIS
9. 180 DID
10. 168 LAD
11. 126 HAS, ADO, ASH
12. 122 ALL, HAY
More words: DAY, SAY, SHY, LAY, ASH, ASS, DISH, HALL, DASH …

5
1. 2
2. 55
3. 28 000
4. 100 grams (or 100 g)
5. 1/10
6. 9
7. 24
8. 500 millilitres (500 ml)
9. 72 hours
10. 1 1/3
11. 15
12. £7.19
13. 9.7
14. 1/3

6
1. 133
2. 156 miles
3. 43 minutes
4. 4900
5. 1.65 metres (1.65 m), or 165 centimetres (165 cm)
6. 1.25 litres (1.25 l), or 1250 millilitres (1250 ml)
7. 252
8. 280 cm^2
9. 0.03
10. 20 pots

7

+	34	18	25	38	16
19	53	37	44	57	35
48	82	66	73	86	64
53	87	71	78	91	69
37	71	55	62	75	53
26	60	44	51	64	42

8
1. 25 000
2. 75
3. 100 metres (or 100 m)
4. forty thousand six hundred
5. 7
6. 19
7. £20
8. 2.72 metres (or 2.72 m)
9. 255
10. 990 grams (990 g), or 0.99 kilograms (0.99 kg)
11. 1, 42   2, 21   3, 14   6, 7
12. 69
13. 21   14. 0.23

9

	even	divisible by 3	divisible by 5	prime
odd		3, 9, 15, 21, 27	5, 15, 25	3, 5, 7, 11, 13, 17, 19, 23, 29
less than 15	2, 4, 6, 8 10, 12, 14	3, 6, 9, 12	5, 10	3, 5, 7, 11, 13
square	4, 16	9	25	
divisible by 6	6, 12, 18, 24, 30	6, 12, 18, 24, 30	30	
divisible by 4	4, 8, 12, 16, 20, 24, 28	12, 24	20	

22 and 26 will not fit in.

10

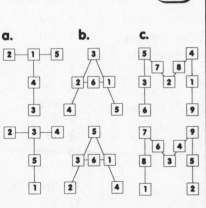

11
1. 25
2. 12
3. £2.75
4. 210 cm^3
5. 60p
6. 9 m^2
7. 26
8. 37
9. 7
10. 40

12
1. 1 3/10
2. 0.3
3. 156
4. 550
5. 63 000
6. 750
7. 668
8. 840
9. 950 millilitres (950 ml), or 0.95 litres (0.95 l)
10. 1 1/5
11. 0.75
12. £4.72
13. 420 minutes
14. 8

13
1. 17
2. 51
3. ten thousand and ten
4. 1, 16   2, 8   4, 4
5. 24
6. 4.1 centimetres (4.1 cm), or 41 millimetres (41 mm)
7. 6100
8. £90
9. 2 1/3
10. 1/4
11. £21.92
12. 770
13. 0.07
14. 1024

14

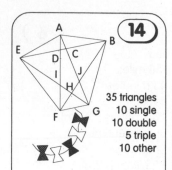

35 triangles
10 single
10 double
5 triple
10 other

ABC	ACE	AGI	BFG	EFH
ABD	ADE	BCG	BGH	EFI
ABE	AEF	BCJ	BGJ	FGH
ABF	AEG	BDF	CEG	FGI
ABG	AEI	BEF	DEF	FGJ
ABJ	AFG	BEG	DEI	FHI
ACD	AFJ	BEH	EFG	GHJ

17

1. 58
2. 156
3. 156
4. 54
5. 0.25
6. 24
7. 150
8. 20
9. 23
10. 6
11. 1.96 kilometres (1.96 km), or 1960 metres (1980 m)
12. 27
13. 144
14. 60

18

1. 5:18 p.m.
2. 30 miles
3. 20
4. 400 m.p.h.
5. £5.55
6. 0.9, 1.5, 1.7, 2.1
7. 50
8. 12
9. 50
10. 3.7 kilograms (3.7 kg)

19

Winston's homework

1. $46 + 98 = 144$
2. $73 - 49 = 24$
3. $225 \times 7 = 1575$
4. $894 \div 6 = 149$

20

1. 416
2. 68
3. 1.64 metres (1.64 m), or 164 centimetres (164 cm)
4. 10
5. ½
6. 5
7. 3⅓
8. 730 or 731 days
9. 10000
10. 1,30 2,15 3,10 5,6
11. 30
12. 75p
13. 9
14. 240

23

1. 86
2. 40p
3. 10:33 p.m.
4. 58%
5. 10
6. 5¼ pints
7. 5 faces
8. 1000080
9. 50
10. 125 miles

24

1. 8
2. 0.07
3. 121
4. 3
5. 480000
6. 0.4
7. £2.27
8. 2.5
9. 4.73 metres (or 4.73 m)
10. 22.5 or 22½
11. ³/₁₀
12. 125
13. 12
14. 1.7

25

1. 5
2. 390
3. 43
4. 7
5. 100
6. 144
7. 6
8. 2⅔
9. 12.1
10. ⁴/₅ or ⁸/₁₀
11. 18
12. 28
13. 150
14. 840

26

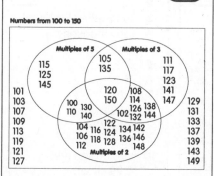

Numbers from 100 to 150

27

1. PEN 126
2. SEA 48
3. NET 162
4. INN 72
5. ASK 40
6. SET 108
7. INK 120
8. PAN 84
9. EAT 216
10. TIN 216
11. PEA 168
12. KIT 360
13. PET 378
14. TAP 252
15. PIN 168
16. TIP 504

More words: APE, SIT, NAP, SIP …

28

For example,

17 − 4	= 13
− 4	= 9
− 4	= 4
− 4	= 1

17 − 5	= 12
× 5	= 60
− 55	= 5
÷ 5	= 1

17 × 6	= 102
− 66	= 36
÷ 6	= 6
÷ 6	= 1

17 × 2	= 34
− 22	= 12
÷ 2	= 6
÷ 2	= 3
− 2	= 1

29

1. 27
2. 25
3. 6
4. 45 millilitres (or 45 ml)
5. 17
6. 114
7. yes - 368 is a multiple of 4
8. 11
9. 70
10. £110
11. ⁶/₁₀ or ³/₅
12. 3.2
13. ⅕
14. 300

30

1. 127
2. ⅕ ½ ⅗ ¾
3. 12
4. 50p
5. 45
6. 342
7. 6 faces
8. 120 hours
9. 45 tenths
10. £72

31

In the cave there are:

25 tarantulas
75 beetles

32

1. ⅜
2. 0.9
3. 551
4. 24
5. 3
6. 19
7. 85p
8. 3
9. 150
10. 40%
11. 7
12. ⁹/₂₄ or ⅜
13. 416
14. ⅕

34

a.	22	APE
b.	26	BEAR
c.	34	CAMEL
d.	37	SEAL
e.	39	EMU
f.	56	WOLF
g.	45	FOX
h.	50	LION

35

1. 286, 141, 573
2. 3.75
3. 36p
4. 140 millilitres (or 140 ml)
5. 800 cm³
6. 11°C
7. 880 centimetres
8. 14
9. 84 days
10. £4.95

36

1. 7.6
2. 18
3. 360
4. 16
5. 1000
6. 144
7. 24
8. ³/₄
9. ¹/₅
10. £6.70
11. 50 000
12. −14
13. 230
14. 4900

37

1. 0.4
2. 94p
3. 15
4. 36
5. 11
6. 4
7. 8.3
8. 400
9. 6³/₅
10. ²/₅
11. 40
12. 17
13. 671
14. 3.2

41

1. 175
2. 500 000
3. 1600
4. 38
5. 6.7
6. 20
7. £2.05
8. 64
9. 1²/₅ or 1⁴/₁₀
10. yes - 243 is a multiple of 3
11. £39.96
12. 0.3 kilograms (or 0.3 kg)
13. 18
14. 85

39

take 4, leave 5 equal

take 6, leave 5 equal

take 8, leave 4 equal

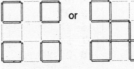 or

take 4, leave 5

take 6, leave 3

take 8, leave 3

  or

take 8, leave 2

42

1. £31.50
2. 34 centimetres (34 cm)
3. 25
4. 47
5. 31
6. £1.90
7. 11, 1, 407
8. ¹/₆ ³/₁₅ ³/₁₀ ²/₅
9. £19
10. 60p

43

There are lots of ways to make 100 with the digits 1 to 9: eg,

123 − 45 − 67 + 89
12 + 3 − 4 + 5 + 67 + 8 + 9
123 + 45 − 67 + 8 − 9
257 − 136 − 9 − 8 − 4
159 + 62 − 34 − 87

Try finding ways that use × as well as + and −: eg,

1 + 2 + 3 + 4 + 5 + 6 + 7 + (8 × 9)
(3 + 4 − 1 − 2) × (6 + 7 + 8 + 9 − 5)

44

1. 13.2
2. 4
3. 350
4. 0.45
5. £2
6. 0.6
7. 125
8. yes - 428 is a multiple of 4
9. 17.8
10. 152
11. 0.7 litres (or 0.7 l)
12. 60%
13. 1.32
14. 8100

47

1. 150 cm²
2. 3.81, 8.13, 8.31, 18.3
3. 8 edges
4. 140 centimetres (140 cm)
5. 7
6. 63
7. 64 minutes
8. ¹/₆
9. ²/₅ or ⁴/₁₀
10. 33¹/₃ %

48

1. 9p
2. 0.37
3. 0.8
4. 2500
5. 0.75
6. 90
7. 647
8. ³³/₅₀ (approximately ²/₃)
9. ¹/₆
10. 0.3
11. 0.95 kilometres (0.95 km)
12. 2994
13. 131
14. 2400

49

1. 4.77
2. 27
3. 425
4. 5634
5. 4926
6. £12
7. 5000
8. 6
9. 4.36
10. £119.94
11. 0.65 metres (or 0.65 m)
12. 1.56
13. 29
14. 67

51

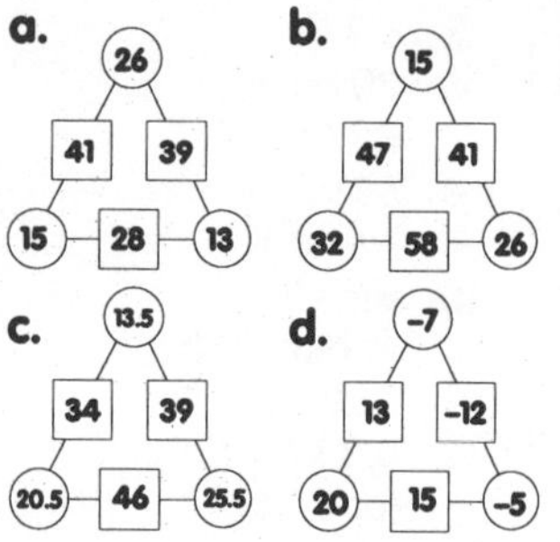
a.
26
41
39
15
28
13
b.
15
47
41
32
58
26
c.
13.5
34
39
20.5
46
25.5
d.
–7
13
–12
20
15
–5

52

+	14	6	17	8	25
19	33	25	36	27	44
28	42	34	45	36	53
7	21	13	24	15	32
9	23	15	26	17	34

×	25	12	20	16	15
4	100	48	80	64	60
6	150	72	120	96	90
3	75	36	60	48	45
8	200	96	160	128	120

53

1 $6\frac{7}{8}$
2 340
3 5.43
4 63
5 5700
6 5
7 4996
8 17.5 or $17\frac{1}{2}$
9 600
10 $1\frac{1}{4}$
11 270
12 638
13 27
14 1 litre is more

54

1 36 miles
2 45 minutes
3 1.7, 1.07, 0.7, 0.17
4 remainder 3
5 12 vertices
6 121
7 1.6 centimetres (1.6 cm), or 16 millimetres (16 mm)
8 96 months
9 0.05 or $\frac{1}{20}$
10 £10.50

56

1 6.5
2 800
3 £40
4 7
5 0.74
6 5343
7 3
8 $\frac{3}{8}$
9 7
10 0.1 kilograms (or 0.1 kg)
11 42
12 31
13 500
14 1.57

57

1

16	2	3	13
5	11	10	8
9	7	6	12
4	14	15	1

2

36	2	3	7	32	31
29	26	13	12	23	8
27	15	20	21	18	10
9	19	16	17	22	28
4	14	25	24	11	33
6	35	34	30	5	1

The magic number is 111.

59

1 211
2 remainder 1
3 £4.80
4 12
5 4 faces
6 81
7 £15
8 $\frac{1}{12}$
9 18
10 0.48

60

1 £72
2 185
3 0.9
4 56
5 3430
6 7.6
7 7
8 0.05 litres (or 0.05 l)
9 7999
10 27
11 $\frac{1}{5}$
12 1 kilometre is less
13 yes - 618 is divisible by 3
14 40

61

1 4.65
2 634
3 70
4 11.5 or $11\frac{1}{2}$
5 0.2
6 37
7 54
8 21 millilitres (or 21 ml)
9 33
10 30 metres (or 30 m)
11 0.1
12 4397
13 24
14 625

62

1 (37 x 21) + 23 = 1000

2 (756 ÷ 18) x 29 = 1218

3 27 + (36 x 18) = 675

4 31 x (87 – 19) = 2108

63

1 34 AS
2 61 IN
3 52 BE
4 25 US
5 43 AM
6 40 IS
7 57 RUB
8 45 SUM
9 81 SEE
10 63 BUN, BIB, BAA, MAM
11 42 BUS
12 84 ARE

More words: ME, AN, INN, ASS, RIM, RIB, BIN, NIB, BAR, RUM …

65

1 85
2 $3\frac{2}{5}$
3 0.15
4 575
5 1316
6 $1\frac{2}{3}$
7 0.05
8 10 000
9 £47.50
10 90
11 355
12 0.02 kilograms (0.02 kg)
13 0.1 or $\frac{1}{10}$
14 $\frac{5}{6}$

66

1 12 edges
2 2 075 006
3 £14.25
4 50
5 14
6 38
7 60
8 55
9 720
10 21 crates

67

largest number
52 x 431 = 22 412

smallest number
13 x 245 = 3185

Change the rules

largest number
632 x 541 = 341 912

smallest number
13 x 2456 = 31 928

68

1 653
2 5
3 0.09
4 $6\frac{1}{3}$
5 1 000 000
6 1327
7 41
8 386
9 0.87 metres (0.87m), or 870 millimetres
10 0.05
11 20
12 0.44
13 8
14 £3.20

69

a. $\frac{1}{4} = 0.25$

b. $\frac{3}{2} = 1.5$

c. $\frac{6}{8} = 0.75$

d. $\frac{7}{2} = 3.5$

e. $\frac{9}{5} = 1.8$

f. $\frac{6}{4} = 1.5$

g. $\frac{9}{6} = 1.5$

h. $\frac{9}{2} = 4.5$

You need pencil and paper. Write only the answers.

1 Which three of these numbers total 1000:   286, 141, 378, 573?

2 What number is half way between 3.7 and 3.8?

3 Oranges cost 45p for 5. How much do 4 oranges cost?

4 By how much is 860 millilitres short of 1 litre?

5 Find the volume of a 10 cm x 10 cm x 8 cm cuboid.

6 The temperature rises by 19°C from –8°C. What is it now?

7 How many centimetres in 8.8 metres?

8 Find the average of 10, 13 and 19.

9 How many days in 12 weeks?

10 11 bags of toffees at 45p each cost … ?

Ask an adult to read these to you.
You need pencil and paper. Write only the answers.

1 10 minus 2.4.

2 Divide 360 by 20.

3 3.6 times 100.

4 Add 9.5 to 6.5.

5 10 cubed.

6 Multiply 48 by 3.

7 Find the sum of 7, 8 and 9.

8 Double three-eighths.

9 Write 0.2 as a fraction.

10 10 times 67p.

11 Half of one hundred thousand.

12 13 minus 27.

13 140 more than 90.

14 Approximately, what is 68 times 72?

Ask an adult to time you.

You need pencil and paper. Write only the answers.

1 $40 \div 100$.

2   10% of £9.40.

3 $889 + \square = 904$.

4 $46 + 18 = 100 - \square$.

5   Add 18 to −7.

6 $5 \times \square \times 6 = 120$.

7 $15 - 6.7$.

8 25×16.

9   Subtract $1\frac{2}{5}$ from 8.

10   What fraction of 1 kg is 400 grams?

11 $\frac{1}{20}$ of 800.

12   Find the average of 20, 25 and 6.

13 $90 + 581$.

14   Write $3\frac{1}{5}$ as a decimal.

38

Shopping

Ask your family to join in.

You need pencil and paper.

Most families buy food and household items each week.

Think of different things your family buys.

Milk is probably one of them.

Beans or rice might be others.

Write a list of 15 different items you might buy.

Discuss with your family what they cost.

Put a price by each one.

Now working by yourself (without a calculator) add up the total cost.

Estimate prices
Total a shopping bill

Square puzzles

Do this by yourself.

You need pencil and paper and 24 matches or cocktail sticks.

Arrange 24 matches to make 9 equal squares like this.

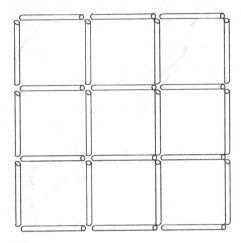

1   Remove 4 matches and leave 5 equal squares.

Remove 4 matches and leave 5 squares, not necessarily equal.

2   Remove 6 matches and leave 5 equal squares.

Remove 6 matches and leave 3 unequal squares.

3   Remove 8 matches and leave 4 equal squares.

Remove 8 matches and leave 3 squares, not necessarily equal.

Remove 8 matches and leave 2 unequal squares.

Sketch what you did in each case.

Now ask your family to try.

Recognise different shapes made of squares
Think logically and visualise rearrangements

Three digits

Two, three or four people can play.

You need a pack of playing cards.

Use the ace to 9 of each suit.

Each player needs pencil and paper.

Shuffle the cards and put them face down in a pile.

Take turns to turn over three cards.

Use them to write two three-digit numbers.

With 6, 5 and 4, say, you could make 654, or 546 or 456 or …

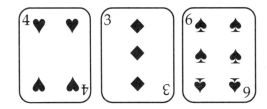

Find the difference between your two numbers.

Try to do this in your head then write it on your paper.

The player who makes the biggest difference scores a point .

When all the cards are turned over, shuffle them and make another pile.

Play at least 10 rounds.

The winner is the player who gets the most points.

Change the rules

The winner is the player who gets the least number of points.

Subtract a pair of three-digit numbers
Understand place value

Ask an adult to read you these.
You need pencil and paper. Write only the answers.

1	7 times 25.	**8**	Four cubed.
2	Half of one million.	**9**	Double seven tenths.
3	40 squared.	**10**	Is 243 a multiple of 3?
4	Take 68 from 106.	**11**	4 shirts at £9.99 each cost … ?
5	Divide 67 by 10.	**12**	Write 300 grams in kilograms.
6	Multiply 0.2 by 100.	**13**	450 divided by 25.
7	10 per cent of £20.50.	**14**	What must be added to 725 to make 810?

You need pencil and paper. Write only the answers.

1 A £35 coat has 10% off in a sale. What does it cost?

2 What is the perimeter of a 8 cm by 9 cm rectangle?

3 What is the difference between –6 and 19?

4 Round 46.7 to the nearest whole number.

5 A number taken from 25 leaves –6. What is the number?

6 What is the cost of 50 cm of lace at £3.80 a metre?

7 One factor of 407 is 37. What are the others?

8 Write in order, largest first: $\frac{2}{5}$, $\frac{3}{10}$, $\frac{1}{6}$, $\frac{3}{15}$.

9 Decrease £20 by 5%.

10 Pears cost 72p for 6.
What do 5 pears cost?

Make 100

Start this on your own.

You need paper, a pencil and some scissors.

Make 9 number cards.

$$\boxed{1}\ \boxed{2}\ \boxed{3}\ \boxed{4}\ \boxed{5}\ \boxed{6}\ \boxed{7}\ \boxed{8}\ \boxed{9}$$

Arrange your cards and + and – signs to make a sum that equals 100.

Use each card once and only once and as many + or – signs as you like.

For example,

$$\boxed{1}\ \boxed{5}\ \boxed{9} + \boxed{6}\ \boxed{4} - \boxed{3}\ \boxed{2} - \boxed{8}\ \boxed{7} = 104$$

Can you do better than this? Ask others to try.

Find different ways to do it.

Add and subtract numbers
Think logically to eliminate what won't work

Ask an adult to time you.

You need pencil and paper. Write only the answers.

1 $4.8 + 8.4$.

2 $168 \div 42$.

3 25×14.

4 $1 - 0.55$.

5 $\frac{1}{20}$ of £40.

6 0.06×10.

7 5^3.

8 Is 428 a multiple of 4?

9 $178 \div 10$.

10 $458 + \square = 610$.

11 Write 700 ml in litres.

12 Write $\frac{3}{5}$ as a percentage.

13 Double 0.66.

14 Approximately, what is 88 x 91?

Stamp cards

Two, three or four people can play.

You need pencil and paper for each player, and a dice.

Each player should draw a stamp card like this.

55p	18p	25p	12p	45p
17p	15p	19p	35p	16p

Take turns to roll the dice.

The dice tells you how many of one stamp you have won.

Choose a stamp on your card and write the total value in the space.

For example, if you throw 4 and choose the 18p space, you win four 18p stamps, and write 72p in the space.

Each space can be used only once.

When all the spaces are full, find the total amount on your card.

The winner is the player with most on their card.

Play several times.

Change the rules

Choose different values for the stamps.

Find multiples of stamp values and their total sum
Understand the relative values and work out a strategy

Emergency call

Two or three people can play.

You need a dice and some beans.

Players may need pencil and paper.

Each player starts with a score of 1.

Take turns to roll the dice.

Multiply your score by the number you rolled.

Try to do this in your head. Use pencil and paper only if you need to.

Record your new score.

Keep going.

The first to reach 999 or more calls it out and wins a bean.

The winner is the first to get 5 beans.

Change the rules

a.   Make the target 9999.

b.   Start with a score of 999 (or 9999) and divide by the number rolled.

Ignore any remainders for your new score.

The first to get a score of less than 1 wins a bean.

Practise short multiplication

You need pencil and paper. Write only the answers.

1   What is the surface area of a 5 cm x 5 cm x 5 cm cube?

2   Write in order, smallest first: 8.13,   18.3,   3.81,   8.31.

3   How many edges has a square-based pyramid?

4   What is the perimeter of a 35 cm by 35 cm square?

5   8 times a number is 4 less than 60. What is the number?

6   The largest factor of 189 is 189. What is the next largest?

7   How many minutes from 14:28 hours to 15:32 hours?

8   Half of one third.

9   Take $^7/_{10}$ from 1$^1/_{10}$.

10 Two-thirds of Sam's books are fiction.
    What percentage is non-fiction?

Ask an adult to read you these.
You need pencil and paper. Write only the answers.

1   15 per cent of 60p.

2   Take 0.63 from 1.

3   Divide 8 by 10.

4   50 squared.

5   Half of 1.5.

6   Multiply 3 by 5 by 6.

7   700 minus 53.

8   Write 0.66 as a fraction.

9   What fraction of £30 is £5?

10 Multiply 0.03 by 10.

11 Write 950 metres in kilometres.

12 3002 take away 8.

13 Increase 87 by 44.

14 Approximately, what is 38 times 62?

Ask an adult to time you.

You need pencil and paper. Write only the answers.

1   10 − 5.23.

2   675 ÷ 25.

3   17 × 25.

4   400 + 5234.

5   5006 − 80.

6   15% of £80.

7   Half of 10 000.

8   8 × □ × 5 = 240.

9   436 ÷ 100.

10   6 tickets at £19.99 each cost … ?

11   Write 65 centimetres in metres.

12   Double 0.78.

13   4 + 7 + 5 + 6 + 7.

14   Decrease 123 by 56.

50

Double or take

Two, three or four people can play.

You need some beans.

The first player chooses a starting number from 50 to 500.

The next player then doubles the number

or   subtracts a square number (1, 4, 9, 16, 25, 36 …)

or   subtracts a cube number (1, 8, 27, 64, 125 …)

The first player to reach zero **exactly** wins a bean.

Take turns to go first.

The winner is the first to get 10 beans.

What is the least number of turns if you start with 1000?

Recognise squares and cubes
Practise doubling and subtraction

Triangle puzzles

Do this by yourself.

You need pencil and paper.

The numbers in the circles have been added in pairs.

The sum of each pair is in the square between the circles.

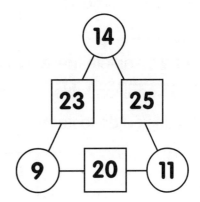

Copy and complete these.

a.

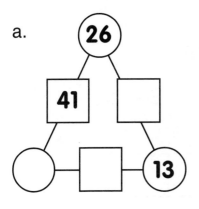

b.

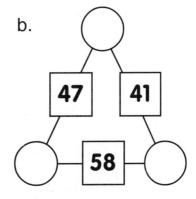

c.

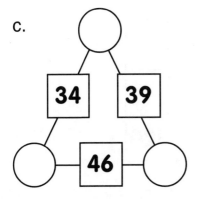

d.

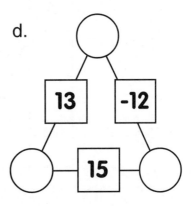

Add and subtract two-digit numbers
Think logically to eliminate what won't work

Fast as you can

Do this by yourself.

You need pencil and paper.

Ask an adult to time you.

Copy and complete these two tables.

One is an addition table. The other is a multiplication table.

Which can you do fastest?

+	14		17		25
19	33				
	42	34			
		13		15	
					34

×		12	20		15
4			80		
	150			96	
	75		60		
					120

Ask an adult to read you these.
You need pencil and paper. Write only the answers.

1   Take 3⅛ from 10.

2   260 more than 80.

3   Divide 543 by 100.

4   9 times 7.

5   Take 400 from 6100.

6   What number cubed equals 125?

7   6 less than 5002.

8   One quarter of 70.

9   What is the product of 25 and 24?

10 Double five eighths.

11 Multiply 9 by 5 by 6.

12 800 subtract 162.

13 How many thirds in 9?

14 Which is more: 1 pint or 1 litre?

You need pencil and paper. Write only the answers.

1   A car's average speed is 48 m.p.h. How far does it go in ¾ hour?

2   How many minutes from 14:17 hours to 15:02 hours?

3   Write in order, largest first: 0.7,   1.7,   1.07,   0.17.

4   What is the remainder when 300 is divided by 9?

5   How many vertices has a hexagonal prism?

6   What is the next square number after 100?

7   Take 34 millimetres from 5 centimetres.

8   How many months in 8 years?

9   One half of one tenth.

10 It costs £1.75 to go skating.
    What do 6 children pay altogether?

55

All the fours

Start this by yourself.

You need pencil and paper and a timer.

List the numbers from 1 to 100.

Set the timer for 15 minutes and start.

$$4 \div \sqrt{4}$$
$$(4 + 4) \times 4$$
$$(44 \div 4) - 4$$

Make each number from 1 to 100.

Use only the digit 4.

Use as many fours as you wish but as few as possible.

You can use any operation (+, −, × or ÷) and the square root sign: $\sqrt{4}$.

Write your calculation next to the number.

Keep going until the timer pings.

Ask your family to join in. Can they make any numbers you have missed?

Can they make any using fewer fours?

Use knowledge of number facts and times-tables
Think flexibly and eliminate what won't work

56

Ask an adult to time you.

You need pencil and paper. Write only the answers.

1   9.2 − 2.7.

2 32×25.

3   5% of £800.

4 $427 \div 61$.

5   Half of 1.48.

6   700 + 4643.

7 $\frac{1}{2} \times 6$.

8   What fraction of 40 ml is 15 ml?

9   49.

10   Write 100 grams in kilograms.

11   7 times 6.

12   8 + 5 + 9 + 3 + 6.

13   Roughly, what is $1992 \div 4$?

14   0.07 + 1.5.

Jigsaws

Do this by yourself.

You need pencil, paper, a ruler and some scissors.

In a magic square each line of numbers (each row, each column, and each of the two long diagonals) adds up to the same magic number.

1   This is a magic square.

Each of the numbers 1 to 16 is used once.

The magic number is 34.

Copy the square carefully and complete it.

	2	3	
5			8
	7	6	
4			1

Now cut your square along the dotted lines.

Shuffle up the four pieces.

Can someone else put them together again?

2   Copy these four pieces carefully, then cut each one out.

17	22	28
24	11	33
30	5	1

36	2	3
29	26	13
27	15	20

9	19	16
4	14	25
6	35	34

7	32	31
12	23	8
21	18	10

Put the pieces together to make a magic square.

What is the magic number?

Add several one- and two-digit numbers
Work systematically

Multiply

Two, three or four people can play.

An adult with a calculator should act as referee.

You each need pencil and paper.

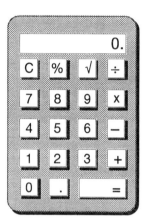

The first player chooses a starting number (say 17).

The second player chooses a larger number (say 90).

Now take turns.

Each say what to multiply the smaller number by to give the larger.

Choose a number with one decimal place like 5.3.

Now do the multiplication: for example, 17 x 5.3 = 90.1.

Record your answer.

The referee checks whether the answers are right.

The player to get closest to the target scores a point.

The winner is the first to get 10 points.

Estimate how many times one number goes into another
Practise multiplication of a decimal by a whole number

You need pencil and paper. Write only the answers.

1   What is the first prime number after 200?

2   What is the remainder when 175 is divided by 6?

3   15 buns at 32p each cost … ?

4   96 children are in 8 equal teams. How many in each team?

5   How many faces has a tetrahedron?

6   Round 80.6 to the nearest whole number.

7   A meal costs £3.75. What do 4 meals cost?

8   One quarter of one third.

9   What is 33⅓ per cent of 54?

10 What number is shown on this scale?

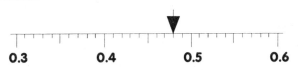

| 0.3 | 0.4 | 0.5 | 0.6 |

Ask an adult to read you these.
You need pencil and paper. Write only the answers.

1   Take 10 per cent off £80.

2   136 plus 49.

3   Divide 90 by 100.

4   8 times 7.

5   Take 600 from 4030.

6   Half of 1.52.

7   Multiply 100 by 0.07.

8   Write 50 millilitres in litres.

9   8005 minus 6.

10 How many quarters in 6¾?

11 One hundredth of 20.

12 Which is less: 1 mile or 1 kilometre?

13 Is 618 divisible by 3?

14 What is the square root of 1600?

Ask an adult to time you.
You need pencil and paper. Write only the answers.

1   20 – 15.35.
2   Add 260 to 374.
3   4900.
4   ½ × 23.
5   Divide 2 by 10.
6   9 + 7 + 6 + 7 + 8.
7   9 times 6.

8   What is 7% of 300 ml?
9   825 ÷ 25.
10 Write 0.03 km in metres.
11 Double 0.05.
12 800 + 3597.
13 12 ÷ ½.
14 25 × 25.

62

Missing signs

Try these by yourself.
You need pencil and paper.

Each box represents a missing sign (+, –, × or ÷).
Can you work out what each box is?

a. $(37 \square 21) \square 223 = 1000$

b. $(756 \square 18) \square 29 = 1218$

c. $27 \square (36 \square 18) = 675$

d. $31 \square (87 \square 19) = 2108$

Estimate and approximate
Use knowledge of number facts and times-tables

Underwater

Ask all your family to join in.

S U B M A R I N E

11 14 17 20 23 26 29 32 35

Add up the numbers standing for the letters.

Find words that are worth these.

Two-letter words

1	34	**4**	25
2	61	**5**	43
3	52	**6**	40

Three letter words

7	57	**10**	63
8	45	**11**	42
9	81	**12**	84

Secretly make another word using the letters of SUBMARINE.

Work out what it is worth and tell everyone.

Can they guess what your word is?

Add two or three two-digit numbers
Use knowledge of addition facts

Fractions

Two, three or four people can play.

You need two dice.

Each player needs pencil and paper.

Each player should draw a strip like this.

Take turns to roll the dice.

If the numbers are the same, roll again to get two different numbers.

Use your two numbers to make a fraction less than 1.

If you roll, say, 4 and 5 you make the fraction ⅘.

Now work out that fraction of 60. This is your score.

Write your score on your strip.

Carry on until your strip is full of numbers.

Now change over strips with someone else.

Take turns to roll the two dice again.

If your score is the same as a number on the grid, cross it out.

Otherwise wait for your next turn.

The first to cross out all their numbers wins.

Change the rules

Work out fractions of 120, 180 or 240 instead of 60.

Find fractions of 60, 120, 180 or 240

Ask an adult to read you these.
You need pencil and paper. Write only the answers.

1   17 times 5.
2   10 minus 6⅗.
3   Half of 0.3.
4   23 times 25.
5   Take 700 from 2016.
6   Double five sixths.
7   5 divided by 100.

8   100 squared.
9   Take 5 per cent off £50.
10 How many halves in 45?
11 295 more than 60.
12 Write 20 grams in kilograms.
13 One hundredth of 10.
14 What fraction of 30 miles is 25 miles?

You need pencil and paper. Write only the answers.

1   How many edges has an octahedron?

2   Write in figures **two million, seventy-five thousand and six**.

3   Tennis balls cost £9.50 for 6. What do 9 tennis balls cost?

4   Round 49.7 to the nearest whole number.

5   Share 84 equally among 6.

6   What is the difference between 87 and 125?

7   Divide 20 by one third.

8   Add up all the whole numbers from 1 to 10.

9   How many hours in September?

10 A crate holds 16 bottles.
    How many crates hold 336 bottles?

Big products

Try this by yourself.

You need pencil and paper.

Each time, use each of these numbers and signs once and only once.

| 1 | 2 | 3 | 4 | 5 | | × | = |

What is the biggest number you can make?

What is the smallest number you can make?

Change the rules

Try with 1, 2, 3, 4, 5 and 6, and × and =.

Practise multiplication
Understand place value and work out a strategy

Ask an adult to time you.

You need pencil and paper. Write only the answers.

1   237 + 416.

2 $12 \times \square \times 5 = 300$.

3 $9 \div 100$.

4 $\frac{1}{3} \times 19$.

5 1000^2.

6 $\square - 600 = 727$.

7 $1025 \div 25$.

8   548 − 162.

9   Take 130 mm from half a metre.

10   Half of 0.1.

11 $5 \div \frac{1}{4}$.

12   0.5 − 0.06.

13   Find the average of 7, 7, 9, 9 and 8.

14   5% of £64.

Missing digits

Do this by yourself.

You need pencil and paper.

Copy and complete these.

Write one digit in each box to show a fraction and its decimal equivalent.

For example, if you use 3, 4, 5 and 7 you would write:

$$\frac{\boxed{3}}{\boxed{4}} = 0.\boxed{7}\boxed{5}$$

a. Use 1, 2, 4 and 5.

$$\frac{\boxed{}}{\boxed{}} = 0.\boxed{}\boxed{}$$

b. Use 1, 2, 3 and 5.

$$\frac{\boxed{}}{\boxed{}} = \boxed{}.\boxed{}$$

c. Use 5, 6, 7 and 8.

$$\frac{\boxed{}}{\boxed{}} = 0.\boxed{}\boxed{}$$

d. Use 2, 3, 5 and 7.

$$\frac{\boxed{}}{\boxed{}} = \boxed{}.\boxed{}$$

e. Use 1, 5, 8 and 9.

$$\frac{\boxed{}}{\boxed{}} = \boxed{}.\boxed{}$$

f. Use 1, 4, 5 and 6.

$$\frac{\boxed{}}{\boxed{}} = \boxed{}.\boxed{}$$

g. Use 1, 5, 6 and 9.

$$\frac{\boxed{}}{\boxed{}} = \boxed{}.\boxed{}$$

h. Use 2, 4, 5 and 9.

$$\frac{\boxed{}}{\boxed{}} = \boxed{}.\boxed{}$$

Recognise equivalent fractions and decimals
Think logically and eliminate what won't work

PUBLISHED BY THE PRESS SYNDICATE OF THE UNIVERSITY OF CAMBRIDGE
The Pitt Building, Trumpington Street, Cambridge CB2 1RP, United Kingdom

CAMBRIDGE UNIVERSITY PRESS
The Edinburgh Building, Cambridge CB2 2RU, United Kingdom
40 West 20th Street, New York, NY 10011-4211, USA
10 Stamford Road, Oakleigh, Melbourne 3166, Australia

First published 1998

Printed in the United Kingdom by Scotprint Ltd, Musselburgh

A catalogue record for this book is available from the British Library

ISBN 0 521 65551X paperback

Cover Illustration by Graham Round
Cartoons by Tim Sell

This book covers:
- reading and writing large numbers
- recognising and using negative numbers
- addition and subtraction of pairs of large numbers, fractions and decimals
- rounding to the nearest 10, 100 or whole number
- tables to 10 x 10
- multiplication and division by 10s and 100s
- finding fractions and percentages
- finding areas, volumes and perimeters
- finding averages
- reading scales
- problems involving money, time or measurement